YOUR BUSINESS HAS NO WORTH

Moe Tabesh, CPA, CGA

Dedication Page

To Bahar, Sara, and Zak

For your unwavering support, endless energy, and the joy you bring to my life.

It had been barely three months since I had been in Washington DC. During this time, my world had been rather quiet, no new adventures. I went about my side business, putting together my 15th Financial Literacy workshop.
What can I say?

It is perhaps my hobby and goal to see that the common man gets a good understanding of his finances, so that he could run his business and home successfully.

I sat in front of my computer screen on a fine spring morning, sipping a cup of coffee. I couldn't stay choked up in my abode when the weather was giving. I sat in my verandah, enjoying the morning sun. The cherry blossoms, and tulips in my front garden had bloomed. It was a fine way to start the month of April.

"Captain! Good morning!" Herschel, my neighbor living across the street, greeted me.
"Good morning, Herschel." I waved back.
"Good morning, sir." His little boy greeted.
"How are you, my boy?" I shouted.
"Doing great, sir." The little boy responded.

"We're going hiking. Why don't you join us?" Herschel invited.

I would have loved to join them, if I loved walking under the sun. But I didn't.
"Thank you, but I've got some work to finish."
They moved along, going about their business, while I did mine. I was happy he didn't press on the invitation. It would have been awkward.

Just then, lost in the sun's vitamin D, an email notification popped up. Curious, I opened it.

It was a business award ceremony invitation. I had been invited to this year's Stevie Awards, as I had been nominated as Accountant of the Year and Financial Adviser of The Decade.

Goodness gracious!

This was such an honor. My hard work was paying off. According to the email, the event was to be held in two weeks in Florida. This meant I had to make plans to travel to Florida.

I waited patiently for the two weeks to run by, so that I could head to Florida to accept my award. I practiced my acceptance speech every day in the bathroom. It was most important that as Captain, I left an accounting pun for my many fans.

Three days before the event, I took a flight to Florida. The usual two hour and thirty minute flight seemed a lot longer due to my air anxiety. Arriving at the airport, I took an Uber to a hotel right by the event venue.

I spent the next two days working harder at my acceptance speech, knowing fully well I had only been nominated, not awarded for certain. For some reason, I was rest assured the award was mine. My work contributions in the last year were not only colossal, but epic as well. I deserved this win.

Oh! The opportunities this will bring. More and bigger clients, maybe even a year-long contract, who knows. This and more were benefits of being an attendee and awardee of such an esteemed event.

The D-Day for the Stevie Awards finally came. As a nominee, I had a reserved seat placed with a group of CPAs just like myself. Some of them were also nominees in the same category. I could sense the high-fly competition, something common among professionals.

Finally, after much talk and ado, the categories for which I had been nominated came. Much to my surprise, I didn't win in both categories. I couldn't see any reason for me losing in the accountancy category or in the financial advisers' category. The competition wasn't fierce in my opinion. I was older and, in fact, more experienced than most others in the category. But with dignity, I took it all in. I had been made an underdog in this industry.

I decided to attend the after party of Stevie Awards for networking purposes. Winning Financial Adviser of the Decade made it a lot easier. I exchanged a lot of contacts that evening, it was amazing.

At nine o'clock that evening, I decided to give myself a little break from socializing. And so, I moved to take some fresh air on the terrace. I sipped my cocktail solely, soaking in my past accomplishments, my present position and what the future possibly held. The full moon gave me hope of many more recognitions to come for the impeccable impact I am yet to make.

"Good evening."

There came a thick voice from behind me. I turned around to see who it was. It was a rather tall man in a well tailored tuxedo. His strong accent gave him away to be of English descent.

"Good evening sir," I responded, unsure of this new acquaintance.

The fine young man walked over, apparently joining me in the cool breeze.

"I am Grant Wellington." He extended his hand for a handshake, obviously expecting me to introduce myself. It was also etiquette, so I did.

"I am Sir. Captain Number Cruncher."

He broke into a wide smile. Of course, he knew me.
"Captain Number Cruncher!" His English voice exclaimed.
"Yes!" I replied, returning the smile.
"Congratulations on your nominations, sir."
"Thank you."
"I must say, I didn't know about you until you were nominated for the Stevie Awards."

My face shone with genuine surprise. Someone in the business field did not know of me. Maybe it is because he is British. Even if you didn't know the name, you ought to know the moniker. It was quite catchy.

"When the nominee list was published," he continued, "I, of course, did my research."
"Oh, wow! What did you find?"
"I found your impressive portfolio on the internet! Your work, oh my!"
Grant was definitely a fan.
"I'm glad I could make such a small impact," I attempted to be modest.

"Small? You really are my financial adviser of the decade. You should have won both categories in my opinion. What was the second one, now? Uhm…the accountant of the year."

There! Someone finally said it. I deserved that win. I knew I did. Good riddance to the politics that might have taken play.

"Tell me, sir." I started, "What do you do for a living."
"Oh! I am a marketing professional."
"Good. Good."

"Yes. I have a business in Amsterdam, although I would like to open a branch here in America."

"That is wonderful."

"It is. The new branch might possibly be in Florida, or in California, whichever has the better market."

"That's a great idea and consideration."

"It is, isn't it?"

I nodded accordingly.

"I wish you good luck in your business venture."

"Thank you. Say, can I have your contact? You know, so that I can reach for some financial advice concerning the business."

"Of course."

Another client! I thought to myself.

"(+1)202 555 1234" I read.

"Thank you."

"It was nice meeting you."

"Nice meeting you too, sir."

A month passed, and I still had not gotten a call or text from Mr. Grant. You would think he had forgotten me, or abandoned his business. Those were the only two fitting reasons I could think of.

Grr Grr!

My phone rang. It was an unknown number. I wondered who it might be, as I rarely get calls from unknown numbers. If need be, an email would have been fine.

"Hello."

"Hello. Good morning."

"Good morning. Who am I speaking with, please?"

Courteousness was important, in case it was a potential client.

"This is Grant Wellington, the professional marketer you had met at the Stevie Awards."

"Oh! Grant!" I remember him alright. A Grant with the impeccable English accent was hard to forget.

"Great! How do you do this fine morning, Captain Cruncher?"
"I'm very well, thank you. How about you?"
"Just fine."

There was a soft pause on the call as I waited for him to get straight to the point - something I like.

"You recall when I collected your contact information at the after party, I said I might need some financial advice sometime?"

"Yes, I recall."

"Well, I do need one now."
"Hmm…okay. Go on." I beckoned.
"I want to get people to invest in my company so I can take on more projects."
"You're referring to the new branch in America, right?"
"Yes, in Florida."
"Congratulations."
"Thank you."
"Hmm hmm. Go on."

"How much do you think I can get from the investors? A hundred thousand, maybe two hundred thousand?"

"I cannot give you a response now. I have to go through your company's financial records properly before I can draw any conclusions or give any advice."
"Ah! Yes, you have a good point."

"So you have no financial advice on how I can draw investors to my company?"
"None for now, sir."
"What do we do now, then?"

I heard him chuckle a little on the phone. He had a good sense of humor.

With a smile, I replied, "It is simple. However, it isn't one that should be discussed over the phone."

"True."

"Do I have to come down to Washington DC?"

"If you can bring with you all your company's financial records, then yes, it is fine." A little sarcasm there didn't hurt.

"I see, then you will come to Florida then."

"It will cost you, my good man."

"It is fine. Send all your charges to me via email, with your account details and flight information, of course. It will all be sorted out."

"Okay, then. It is settled. I will be coming to Florida on Friday."

"Good. I look forward to your coming."

"Okay."

"Thank you, sir."

"You are most welcome."

It was settled. Another adventure awaited me in Florida. I couldn't contain my excitement. Another client whose profit I was going to help them maximize.

I made another two hour and thirty minute flight to Florida, this time strictly for business. Unlike most clients, Grant, himself, received me at the airport. He had booked me a hotel room not far from his company.

"How was the flight to Florida, sir?"

"It was quite alright, although I am jet lagged."

"Nothing a little rest cannot solve."

"Yes, yes."

"So you would be coming tomorrow right?"

"Tomorrow? That is Saturday."

"Yes?"

"It's the weekend. I don't work on weekends. I'll be in your office by 8am sharp on Monday."

Grant wasn't too pleased by the turn of events, but there was nothing I could do. I had to stick to my work ethic.

As agreed, I was at the StrategicEdge Marketing Solutions Inc.

The exterior of the firm was a rather simple one. It exuded a sleek and modern aesthetic, with clean lines and a contemporary design. It was very much expected of a young man like Grant. The building facade featured large windows, with the company's logo prominently displayed near the entrance.

I walked into what I would describe as an epitome of sophisticated professionalism. I was greeted by a spacious and impeccably designed reception area adorned with modern furnishes everywhere.

On the walls, there hung frames of clients' reviews smartly arranged. Frames of quotes and the esteemed StrategicEdge Marketing Solutions teams were also on display.

The overall ambiance was neutral and inviting, with a muted color palette of neutral colors creating a sense of tranquility and focus.

The receptionist, a lady, possibly in her mid-thirties, sat at her station, waving to me to come over for assistance. Well, I didn't need much of her assistance as directions to respective offices and workstations had already been placed beside the elevator and the stairs.

I walked to the elevator, adjacent to the entrance. Grant's office was on the second floor. I took the elevator there, prepping my mind for the long finance lecture I was about to give.

Getting to the second floor, I made a stop at his secretary's office. As part of work etiquette, it was important Grant was informed of my presence before I walked into his office.

"Good   morning."
"Good   morning,
sir."
"I am Captain Number Cruncher."

I introduced myself with pride and dignity.

"Ohh! Yes, my boss informed me of your coming." Her face lit up.
"Is he in?"
"Yes, he is. Uhm…let me inform him that you're here."
"Hmm. Hmm."
"Sir, the Captain Number Cruncher is here." She said over the receiver.
"Send him in, please." Grant replied.
She dropped the receiver, her attention once again on me.
"Sir, you can go in. His office is just beside…."
"I've got it. Thank you." I interrupted. It was already seven minutes past eight o'clock. I didn't want to delay any further.

I opened the door to Grant's exquisite office. He was a man of good taste. Just as I stepped in, a group of people, probably workers, stepped out.

Grant stood from his seat to receive him. He was a real fan.
"Welcome Sir. Cruncher."
"Thank you, Grant. It's a fine office you have here. The building in all, is quite exquisite as well."
We shook hands while Grant maintained what I refer to as a professional blush.
"Thank you. It's all hard
work." "Hmm Hmm, yes it
is."
We both took our seats, ready to get down to business.

"Those contain the financial records of StrategicEdge Marketing Solutions Inc." He said pointing
to a small envelope placed on the left side of the table.

" It was the HR team that just stepped as you came in."

"Ohh, alright." I replied, now placing my laptop on the table. I didn't have the energy for small
talk now, I needed to focus on the job I was here to do.

For about forty five minutes, I studied the financial records and trends it took. I could say the
state of the business wasn't so bad for I had seen far worse in all my years of practice.

Either way, there was a clear need for an improvement and step up in the way the business was
managed. If not, StrategicEdge Marketing Solutions would become one of the far worse I have
seen.

Grant sat opposite me, going about his own business while he waited for me to finish with my
inspection and analysis. He looked up from his tablet at intervals to get a glimpse of what I was
up to.

Finally, I cleared my throat to signify that I was done.
"Grant, I am done with your records."
"Okay."

"Now, we can
talk."
"Hmm…thank
you."
We both paused, taking sips out of our cups of coffee. The real business was about to begin.
"So, on the phone, I asked you a question."
"Yes, you did. Please, repeat the question."

'I want to get people to invest in my company so I can take on more projects. How much do you
think I can get? 100K, 200K?"

“Yes. I believe my answer is zero dollars.”
“Zero? How is that possible?”

Grant's eyes widened. He was surprised. He stared at me, anticipating the reason for my peculiar answer.

His nervous face relaxed into a smile. I smiled back and replied,

"Yes, you will get nothing more than zero dollars from your

investors." "How so, Captain?"

"It is a rather simple matter," I replied.

"It doesn't seem so simple to me. What could cause me to get absolutely nothing from investors?"

"Hmm…let's take a look at your business, shall we?"

"Yes, we shall." He replied, his English accent being prudish.

I turned over my computer system to face him.

"From your records, we can see that you earn fifteen thousand dollars as the owner of the company."

Grant nodded in agreement. His earnings were rather low for a professional marketer like himself. But, I planned to keep that to myself for the moment. We would get to that in time.

"We can also see from the records, that you take out a dividend of five thousand dollars. Did you not?"

"Yes, I did." He replied, this time puzzled. He may have thought he had done something wrong.

"Do you know that taking dividends reduces the amount of profit retained within the company for reinvestment or other purposes?"

Grant remained silent. However, I continued.

"Do you know this could impact the company's ability to fund future growth initiatives or handle unforeseen expenses?"

The silence in the room became loud, but I was only just starting.

"This low retained earnings is one of the reasons why you now need investors in the company."

"I agree but …."

"Grant, please let me finish, I am about to make a point. I'd give you the opportunity to speak in due time."

We exchanged tensed smiles. Then, the conversation continued.

"I would like you to know that dividends also affect the cash flow rate of a firm. It's essential to ensure that the company maintains sufficient cash reserves to meet operational needs and financial obligations. This you must always bear in mind."

"Noted."

"Now, I will give you my number one justification for saying you will get only zero dollars from your investors."

"I'm all ears."

"How is it possible that you, sir, the owner of StrategicEdge Marketing Solutions, a master marketing professional, earns only twenty thousand dollars in total?"

"This is what the corporation can afford."

"Exactly my point."

Grant stared at the computer screen a little, trying to grasp what I insinuated.

"This corporation can only afford to pay 20K in compensation. That is really low, don't you think?"

"Yes, it is. But at this point,it is what we can afford. Anything beyond that will affect the company negatively, truth be told."

"Listen, the cash flow of your company is bad."

There was a dead silence from Grant. I continued anyway because I needed him to listen now,not talk.

"The bank balance is almost a thousand dollars. You also have a balance on the company's credit card. This means that in total, you have a negative cash balance. Were you aware of this?"

"I was aware of the company's cash flow. But, I wasn't informed we had a negative balance."

I remained silent for a minute, letting reality sink into Grant's mind.

"Tell me, Grant." I began, "would you ever consider investing in a company that had a negative balance, or even a zero balance?"

Grant's silence elongated.

"The truth is you wouldn't even give it a thought if the balance were below five hundred dollars, not to speak of a negative balance. I wouldn't even blame you for such choices because it is very practical."

I told my clients' the truth in words, clear and still. Grant's case wasn't going to be any different. At this juncture, his business had no worth whatsoever. No sane investor would put his money in such a business.

"Can I ask you something, Grant?" I asked.

"Yes, please. Go ahead."

"What exactly is your reason for giving the owner of StrategicEdge Marketing Solutions only twenty thousand dollars as reimbursement?"

"Hmm…" Grant began, "I am of the notion that taking a high salary is that if the investors come and see that he earned $100K, they will not trust the company."

"Really? Are you sure about this?"

I needed Grant to think clearly on his stance on this matter.

"Let us be realistic, Cruncher. Wouldn't potential investors think that I am greedy if I earned such an amount of money?"

"Why would they?"

"They would think that I am taking lots of money. "

"Grant."

"Captain."

I stopped to take sips of coffee, but it was already cold and distasteful.

"Can I have a bottle of water?"

"Okay, I'd request for some."

"Sarah, please get me two bottles of water. Thank you." He requested over the telecom. In five minutes, Sarah, his secretary, was in his office with two bottles of water.

"Thank you, Sarah." We chorused in unison.

I took large gulps of my water, while she cleared the cups of coffee from the table. Now, after our very much needed five minute break, we took off from where we left off.

"Grant, take for instance I'm one of your potential investors."

"Okay."

"Well, I would want to see you making at least a hundred thousand dollars."

I placed my bottle of water on the table, and waited for his response.

"I don't think that's very realistic."

"Hmm…" I took a thinking stance. How do I make Grant see things from a practical investor's point of view?

"Let's be realistic here, Grant."

"Please."

"How much do you believe a person of your qualifications will earn ordinarily, without owning any company."

"It depends on the company."

"Uhmm…let's say a Search Engine Optimization company hires you to lead their marketing team."

"Okay…I would say the salary range should be between a hundred thousand dollars to a hundred and fifty thousand dollars."

"Exactly."

"Hmm."

"So Grant, do you think it is okay for you to be paid only a fifth of a substantial salary in your own company."

"Yes."

"Why?"

"Compared to StrategicEdge Marketing Solutions Inc., those companies are bigger and have more clients and can afford to pay that kind of salary."

"Are you aware of the sort of impression your current salary would give investors?"

"I believe they should think that my decision to prioritize the growth and success of my own company over maximizing personal income in the short term suggests a strategic and forward-thinking approach to entrepreneurship."

"Not at all, Grant."

Grant's demeanor rested in a confused state.

"Your current salary leaves a perception of poor financial health of StrategicEdge Marketing Solutions Inc."

"How so?"

"Investors may view the company's decision to pay below-market salaries as a sign of financial strain or inefficiency."

Grant seemed to take this in well, so I continued.

"The truth is investors may question why the company is unable or unwilling to pay competitive salaries, leading to concerns about the company's profitability and sustainability. When sustainability is questioned, it doesn't do good for the company."

"I see your point now." Grant replied.

"Oh! I have many more points to make."

We both chuckled, gulping our bottles of water.

"Are you aware that a lack of competitive compensation makes it challenging for a company to recruit skilled professionals and retain them?"

"Grant nodded in agreement."

“This will however hinder the company from achieving its set goals.”

“Yes, it will.”

“This is another valid point investors will consider before putting their hard-earned money in your firm.”

Like other clients, Grant had gotten to the point where he began to take notes. This meant I had made progress with him.

“These points I have given, Grant, are all reasons your potential investors will question your competency as the manager of StrategicEdge Marketing Solutions. And really, you do not want them questioning such a sensitive issue.”

“I do not want that.”

“Exactly! I love that you are being honest with me.”

“Thank you.”

“Now, you see the reason why you need to step up the reimbursement you give yourself.”

“Captain, I understand your point very clearly.”

“I'm glad you do.”

“But….”

“There's always a 'but'.” I thought.

“The reason why these other companies can afford to pay up to a hundred thousand dollars or even more to professional marketers like myself is because they are bigger.”

“Bigger? Really?”

“Yes, bigger. They have more clients. That is why they are able to afford such a salary.”

Fairly speaking, Grant had a good point. But then again, he wasn't seeing this issue from a wider point of view. Expanding his perspective of finance was my job. So I did it.

“Grant, do you know that none of these big companies we have now started as they are now.”

He fell silent. I hit the truth he had overlooked.

"You do know what I mean, don't you?" "I do."

"The well-known Apple Inc. we know of today was founded by Steve Jobs. May I remind you of how it all started?"

"Yes, you may."

"The humble beginnings of Apple Inc. can be traced back to the garage of Steve Jobs' childhood home, where Jobs and Wozniak began building and selling personal computers."

Grant nodded, following the story.

"The first product developed by Apple was the Apple I, a single-board computer kit. Steve Wozniak designed the hardware, while Steve Jobs handled the marketing and sales. They had only themselves on the team. They initially built the computers by hand."

"That's inspiring but not exactly my case now."

"It is Grant." I replied, placing my hand on his hand, trying my best to be persuasive.

"Grant, from those humble beginnings in a garage, Apple continued to grow and innovate, introducing groundbreaking products such as the Macintosh, iPod, iPhone, and iPad, which revolutionized the consumer electronics market. Today, Apple is one of the most valuable and influential companies in the world."

"Apple is one in a thousand companies, Captain."

"Apple isn't the only company with humble beginnings. What about Google?"

"I haven't heard the story of Google."

"Then I must tell you."

I cleared my throat, preparing myself for another tale of grass to grace.

"Google was founded by Larry Page and Sergey Brin, two Ph.D. students at Stanford University, in 1998. It was a mare research Project Page and Brin began while they were graduate students."

"Was a garage involved?" Grant smirked, disbelievingly.

But he was in for a surprise.

"Yes. Initially, Google operated out of a small garage in Menlo Park, California, which belonged to Susan Wojcicki, who later became the CEO of YouTube."

"Wow!"

"Yes! Google's breakthrough came when it officially launched its search engine website, google.com. Google's relentless focus on innovation, user experience, and technology has propelled it to become one of the most valuable and influential companies in the world, shaping the way people access and interact with information online. Everyone uses Google. I use Google. You use Google. But, it all started small."

"I get your point, Captain."

"The key thing about these companies is that they respected the matrix and market values. In fact, they still do. That's how they keep growing."

"Hmm."

"There's a lot you can learn from these companies. They prioritize understanding and meeting the needs of their customers, investing heavily in market research. They make their products and services accessible and easy to use."

"I do all these at StrategicEdge Marketing Solutions, at least, to the best of our abilities."

"Yes you do but are you building a strong brand? Do you have a solid customer base? Do you have a sustainable business model that will continue to drive growth in the long run?"

"We are working on all these."

"But on this path, you are very unlikely to achieve them."

Grant remained silent.

"The ideal thing about these companies is that they not only respected the market value of the company and its products. They also respected the market value of themselves."

"This is about the pay, right?"

"It has always been about the pay, Grant."

"Okay then, Captain. If I decided to raise my reimbursement, how would I go about it?"

Finally, he was asking the real question.

"Looking at your records, Grant," I began, "It is quite obvious that your clients' are highly undercharged."

"Yes. I have a good reason for that."

"Tell me, Grant. Tell me why you think it is okay to offer quality services at an extremely low rate."

I tried to sound sarcastic but held as much seriousness in my voice.

"Remember what you said about building a loyal customer base."

"I do. It is an important feat for every firm or company."

I sensed what point he was getting to, but I wanted to let me finish. It would have been too rude to jump into conclusions -even though such conclusions are a hundred percent accurate.

"Well, now that StrategicEdge Marketing Solutions is still in a medium scale and well on its way to higher grounds…."

"I wouldn't say 'well'." I thought to myself.

"I understand the importance of this large and loyal customer base."

"You still haven't made your point clear, Grant."

"Look, Captain, I believe that a solid customer base can be developed with our pricing system. Clients' are attracted to our very affordable prices."

"Affordable and cut-rate are two entirely different things. You are basically giving away your services for free."

"For now, soon our prices will go up." Grant replied.

"When, Grant?" It was a rhetorical question, requiring no response.

"As far as I know, in all my years of experience," I continued, "Customers are never ready for a jerk in the price of products or services."

Grant fell silent.

IT HAD BEEN BARELY THREE MONTHS SINCE I HAD BEEN IN WASHINGTON DC...

WE'RE GOING HIKING WHY DON'T YOU JOIN US?
THANK YOU, BUT I'VE GOT SOME WORK TO FINISH.

JUST THEN, LOST IN THE SUN'S VITAMIN D, AN EMAIL NOTIFICATION POPPED UP...
YOU HAVE BEEN NOMINATED FOR THE STEVIE AWARDS

AND THE WINNER IS...
...NOT CAPTAIN NUMBER CRUNCHER.

HOW MUCH DO YOU THINK I CAN GET FROM THE INVESTORS?

ZERO DOLLARS.

I AGREE BUT...
GRANT, PLEASE LET ME FINISH, I AM ABOUT TO MAKE A POINT.
I'D GIVE YOU THE OPPORTUNITY TO SPEAK IN DUE TIME.

I WOULD LIKE YOU TO KNOW THAT DIVIDENDS ALSO AFFECT THE CASH FLOW RATE OF A FIRM.
IT'S ESSENTIAL TO ENSURE THAT THE COMPANY MAINTAINS SUFFICIENT CASH RESERVES TO MEET OPERATIONAL NEEDS AND FINANCIAL OBLIGATIONS.
THIS YOU MUST ALWAYS BEAR IN MIND.

NOTED.
NOW, I WILL GIVE YOU MY NUMBER ONE JUSTIFICATION FOR SAYING YOU WILL GET ONLY ZERO DOLLARS FROM YOUR INVESTORS.
I'M ALL EARS.

HOW IS IT POSSIBLE THAT YOU, SIR, THE OWNER OF STRATEGICEDGE MARKETING SOLUTIONS, A MASTER MARKETING PROFESSIONAL, EARNS ONLY TWENTY THOUSAND DOLLARS IN TOTAL?"
THIS IS WHAT THE CORPORATION CAN AFFORD.
EXACTLY MY POINT.
LISTEN, THE CASH FLOW OF YOUR COMPANY IS BAD.
THERE WAS A DEAD SILENCE FROM GRANT.
I CONTINUED ANYWAY BECAUSE I NEEDED HIM TO LISTEN NOW, NOT TALK.

TELL ME, GRANT.
TELL ME WHY YOU THINK IT IS OKAY TO OFFER QUALITY SERVICES AT AN EXTREMELY LOW RATE.
UH... REMEMBER WHAT YOU SAID ABOUT BUILDING A LOYAL CUSTOMER BASE?
YOU ARE BASICALLY GIVING AWAY YOUR SERVICES FOR FREE.
I UNDERSTAND.
AFFORDABLE AND CUT-RATE ARE TWO ENTIRELY DIFFERENT THINGS.
GRANT, DO YOU KNOW THAT SOME OF YOUR CLIENTS MAY CONSIDER YOUR SERVICES TO BE LOW QUALITY BECAUSE YOUR PRICES DO NOT TALLY WITH THE MARKET COMPETITIVE PRICES?

YOU NEED A LOYAL CUSTOMER BASE, YEAH?
YES, I DO.
GRANT, DO YOU KNOW THAT NONE OF THESE BIG COMPANIES WE HAVE NOW STARTED AS THEY ARE NOW.
I HADN'T THOUGHT ABOUT IT LIKE THAT BEFORE.
THE KEY THING ABOUT THESE COMPANIES IS THAT THEY RESPECTED THE MARKET VALUE OF THEM-SELVES.

LOOKING AT YOUR RECORDS, GRANT, IT IS QUITE OBVIOUS THAT YOUR CLIENTS ARE HIGHLY UNDERCHARGED.
YES, I HAVE A GOOD REASON FOR THAT.
OKAY THEN, CAPTAIN. IF I DECIDED TO RAISE MY REIMBURSEMENT, HOW WOULD I GO ABOUT IT?
GRANT, YOU DO NOT WANT THEM QUESTIONING SUCH A SENSITIVE ISSUE.
I WON'T LET THAT HAPPEN.

YES, BRAND IDEN-TITY.
YOU NEED TO ESTABLISH YOUR BUSINESS AS A REPUTABLE AND RELIA-BLE PROVIDER IN THE INDUSTRY...
UHM...WHAT HAPPENS WHEN OUR COMPETITORS OFFER LOWER PRICES?
I BELIEVE IN ALL, WHAT YOU ARE SAYING IS THAT I NEED TO REASSESS THE COMPANY'S PRI-CING STRATEGY...
...FOCUS ON DELIVERING HIGH-QUALITY SERVICES, AND BUILD A STRONG BRAND BASED ON REPUTATION AND RELIABILITY.
WHILE IT IS IMPORTANT TO ENSURE THAT YOUR PRICES ALIGN WITH MAR-KET PRICES AND THAT OF YOUR COMPE-TITORS...
BRAND IDENTITY
...IF YOUR SER-VICES ARE OF HIGHER QUALITY THAN OTHERS IN THE BUSINESS, THEN YOU MAY SET YOUR PRICE HIGHER.

SHOULD THE FIRM GIVE ROOM FOR PRICE NEGOTIATION WITH THE CLIENTS?

GIVING ROOM FOR PRICE NEGOTIATION CAN BE A STRATEGIC DECISION FOR THE FIRM...

....ENSURE THAT THE FIRM REMAINS FINANCIALLY VIABLE.

ON RARE OCCASIONS WITH CLIENTS WHO HAVE PROVEN TO BE LOYAL CUSTOMERS...

EXACTLY.
GOOD MARKETING STRATEGY.

NOW THAT WE WOULD BE IN- CREASING OUR PRICES, HOW CAN WE JUSTIFY THE PRICE INCREASE TO OUR EXISTING CLIENTS?

WHEN NOTIFYING YOUR CLIENTS OF THE INCREASE IN PRICE, THE FIRST THING YOU MUST DO IS TO HIGHLIGHT THE ADDITIONAL VALUE AND BENEFITS...

....ENSURE THAT YOU ARE CLEAR IN YOUR COMMUNICATION.

HOW DO I DO THIS?

BRAND IDENTITY
BY DEMON- STRATING IM- PROVED RE- SULTS.
CASE STUDIES, TESTIMONIALS, OR DATA DEMONSTRATING THE IMPACT OF THE FIRM'S SERVICES ON CLIENTS' BUSINESSES...

YOU HAVE NOT FOUND YOUR IDEAL CLIENT, GRANT.
BRAND IDENTITY

WHO, THEN, IS THE IDEAL CLIENT...
...FOR STRATEGIC EDGE MARKETING SOLUTIONS INC?

THE IDEAL CLIENTS FOR STRATEGIC EDGE MARKETING SOLUTIONS ARE LIKELY GROWTH-ORIENTED BUSINESSES...
ENTITY

NOTED, SIR.

FOCUS ON ATTRACTING AND SERVING YOUR IDEAL CLIENTS CAN LEAD TO MORE SUCCESSFUL...
...AND FULFILLING PARTNERSHIPS IN THE LONG RUN.
BRAND IDENTITY

HMM... YOU MUST BE INTENTIONAL ABOUT ALL OF THIS.
AND ABOVE ALL, AS THE OWNER OF STRATEGIC EDGE MARKETING SOLU-TIONS...
...YOU MUST ENSURE THAT EVERY WORKER, INCLUDING YOUR-SELF, RECEIVES THE APPRO-PRIATE REIMBURSEMENT FOR THEIR JOB.
THANK YOU, CAPTAIN. I WILL APPLY EVERYTHING WE HAVE TALKED ABOUT TODAY.
NOW, GRANT, LIGHTEN UP. YOU DO NOT NEED ALL THIS WORRYING.
WHAT BRIGHT SIDE, CAPTAIN? I DO NOT SEE ONE IN OUR PRESENT CIRCUM-STANCE.
YOU HAVE ME.
INQUIRING MY EXPERTISE ON THIS MATTER HAS BASICALLY SAVED YOUR BUSINESS.
I SEE.

GRANT, CAN I ENGAGE YOU IN A... A... A STORY?"
A STORY?
I ONCE HAD A CLIENT. FOR CONFIDENTIALITY'S SAKE, WE'LL CALL HIM ALEX.
ALEX WAS AN EXQUISITE CHEF ONE OF THE FINEST YOU WOULD SEE IN LONDON.
WHENEVER ALEX PUT ON ONE HAT, HE COMPLETELY NEGLECTED HIS OTHER DUTIES...
...FOCUSING FULLY ON THE DUTY THE CURRENT HAT REPRESEN- TED."
SO, I WAS THIS 'ALEX' YOU SPOKE OF.
YES, YOU WERE.

GRANT, DO NOT THINK YOU ARE THE ONLY PERSON WHO STRUGGLES IN THIS AREA.
TRUST ME, IT IS A GLOBAL DILEMMA.
I SEE.
THANKS.
THINK ABOUT IMPROVEMENT. PEOPLE IM-PROVE.
I WILL.
I REALLY HOPE SO.
IT WAS YET ANOTHER SUCCESSFUL ADVENTURE FOR ME, CAPTAIN NUMBER CRUNCHER.
YOUR BUSINESS WORTH CRAP
STORY: MOETABISH   PENCIL/INK: NOVAL HERNAWAN

"You are building your customer base off of cut-rate prices. This is risky for the business. You talk of raising the prices soon but with the way things are you may never raise them. This is especially because your clients are loyal because of your prices, and not the quality of your work."

I had just begun another lecture on pricing.

"The truth is, by the time you raise your prices appropriately, most of your clients, whether or not they know that it is only right, will still be unhappy at your new price."

Grant had begun to see my point in all of this.

"Now that I have made a mistake, how do I rectify it?"

"Hmm."

I took a sip of my water, rolling up sleeves for the AC to cool off the heat I suddenly felt over

me. "You need a loyal customer base, yeah?"

"Yes, I do."

"Hmm hmm…but you need a customer that is loyal because they know that you will always deliver quality services to them irrespective of your price."

"Okay…."
"Yes, you do."

"I

understand."

"Grant?"

"Captain?"

"Grant, do you know that some of your clients may consider your services to be low quality because your prices do not tally with the market competitive prices?"

"I did not know that."

"But it is true. It's human rationale. A lot of people believe that prices are high quality because the prices are high."

"It does make sense."

"Yes, it does. Although, I am not insinuating that you overprice your services to give the impression that it is high quality."

Grant chuckled. He may have had the thought in his mind. I was glad I had uprooted it.

"Charge your customers appropriately, in a manner that will enable you to receive the right reimbursement as the owner of the company."

"Noted." He replied.

Of course, he had taken notes, ones I expected him to apply. "I

have a question, Captain?"

"Ask away."

"Wouldn't some of my current customers leave due to my new prices?"

"Unfortunately, yes, they would."

Grant's face fell.

"Don't let that bother you. Those customers were never loyal to begin with. Rather, they wanted to take advantage of your pricing. Build a solid brand and a solid customer base follows."

"Hmm hmm."

"Does that answer your question?"

"Yes, it does. Thank you."

"If you were charging the correct amount, then you as an employee would have earned more income which would be inline with the market."

"Okay."

"Do not ever give room for clients to undermine the quality of services provided by your company. Your brand identity matters a lot. It is what pulls the customers in the first instance."

"Brand identity?"

"Yes, brand identity. You need to establish your business as a reputable and reliable provider in the industry, attracting clients who value quality over affordability. Emphasis on reputable and reliable."

Grant nodded. I knew he may be overwhelmed with the amount of knowledge he had to take in. It was an eye opener, after all.

"To show your clients that you care and that you take them into consideration, you may have to raise your prices gradually to reflect the value delivered by the company."

"I believe in all, what you are saying is that I need to reassess the company's pricing strategy, focus on delivering high-quality services, and build a strong brand based on reputation and reliability." Grant replied.

"Exactly." I nodded.

I had hit the nail hard on the head. He had gotten the message, crystal clear.

"Do you have any questions before we move forward?"

"I do, quite a few."

"We should get started then."

"Yes. Yes, we should."

"Your first question?"

"Uhm…What happens when our competitors offer lower prices?"

I snickered. Grant had asked an unexpected but thoughtful question. In the past, I had experienced cases where competitors' prices were reduced a little while after my client raised his.

What would be the solution then?

"While it is important to ensure that your prices align with market prices and that of your competitors, you must also set your pricing strategy confidently based on the quality of the services you provide."

"Okay …it's not such a huge problem."

"No…it's not. If your services are of higher quality than others in the business, then you may set your price higher."

“Okay, understood. Thanks.”

“You're most welcome, Grant.” I responded.

“Now, for my next question, still on this pricing strategy.”

“Should the firm give room for price negotiation with the clients?”

“Hmm…now this is a tough one.”

“I know right. I have pondered on the issue for quite some time.”

“Really?”

“Yeah… even with the low price, some clients still attempt to haggle the price

down.” I laughed for a moment.

“You see what I said about those clients being only interested in your low prices.”

“I do now.”

“Good… back to your question.”

“Yes, please.”

“Giving room for price negotiation can be a strategic decision for the firm, but it should be approached with caution and careful consideration of the potential implications.”

“Implications like what?”

“When price negotiation goes too far, it can compromise the firm's profitability or undermine the value of its services. This is why it is important to establish a minimum acceptable price below which negotiations cannot go to ensure that the firm remains financially viable.”

“I see your point.”

“It is best for the company to consider whether allowing price negotiation aligns with its value proposition and brand positioning. I usually don't advise giving room for negotiation on a regular basis.”

“When is it appropriate then?”

"On rare occasions with clients who have proven to be loyal customers. That's what I call long-term customer privileges."

"Oh wow! Good marketing strategy."

I smiled to myself, rest assured that it was.

"Thank you very much, Captain. You have answered my questions well."

"I'm happy I was able to."

"I must say, I have one last question."

"That's no problem, ask away."

"Now that we would be increasing our prices, I believe our existing clients deserve an explanation for the sudden development."

"Of course, they do. Offering them an explanation ensures a good customer relationship."

"How then can we justify the price increase to our existing clients?"

"This is a thoughtful question, I must say."

"Thank you, Captain."

"When notifying your clients of the increase in price, the first thing you must do is to highlight the additional value and benefits that clients will receive as a result of the price increase."

"Okay…."

"You must let your clients know how the new prices allow business to operate more smoothly and suitably for everyone, best to their favor. Ensure that you are clear in your communication."

"Noted."

"Grant, you must be careful not to create the perception that the services being provided before were of low quality. Rather, you must confer it as an upgrade of the services provided before."

"How do I do this?"

"You can do this by demonstrating improved results. Provide evidence of how the price increase will lead to improved outcomes for the client. Take for instance, the testimonials we have outside at the reception."

“What about them?”

“You can do something like that to demonstrate the improved results. Case studies, testimonials, or data demonstrating the impact of the firm's services on clients' businesses could be highly effective.”

“Okay. I will bear these in mind.”

“Above all, ensure that there is transparent communication between you and your clients. That is the most important. As a brand, you must be approachable. Clients should be free to ask questions and air their opinions respectfully.”

“You have answered all my questions, Captain. And you have done well.”

“I am happy with our progress, but I must say, we're not done.”

“What's left? We have looked through the records, pointed out the necessary and you have made insightful corrections.”

“Yes, we have covered a lot of grounds. But, all this talk about clients has made one thing clear.”

“Which is?”

“You have and are still going after the wrong clients.”

“I am?”

“How so?”

“You have not found your ideal client, Grant.”

Grant remained silent, possibly pondering on who an ideal client is. I decided to pop the question.

“Who is your ideal client, Grant?”

“Captain, this may sound embarrassing but I have never really thought of this.”

“It isn't embarrassing, Grant. It's alright.”

“I always thought whoever thought to patronize my company was a fine client indeed.”

“No, Grant. It is not that simple.”

“It really isn't, isn't it?”

“Yes, Grant. It's beyond the blacks and whites of transactions. You need to know who the ideal client for StrategicEdge Marketing Solutions Inc. is.”

“Who, then, is the ideal client for StrategicEdge Marketing Solutions Inc?”

“The ideal clients for StrategicEdge Marketing Solutions are likely growth-oriented businesses that are looking to expand their customer base, increase brand awareness, and drive revenue growth.”

“Hmm….”

“An ideal client is willing to invest in marketing to achieve their business objectives and is open to innovative strategies and approaches. Such a client knows the value of your services and is willing to appreciate it through a proper compensation.”

“Okay.”

“Clients who undermine your services, and still expect you to deliver are not your ideal clients. You need clients who are collaborative and responsive partners who value communication, transparency, and a proactive approach. They should be willing to work closely with the agency to develop and execute marketing strategies tailored to their specific goals and objectives.”

“Noted, sir.” Grant responded.

“Grant, may I be excused?”

“Huh?”

“I need a bathroom break,” I replied, pointing to the male lavatory.

In about ten minutes, I was back from my break, ready to take off from the break in transmission.

“Where were we?” I inquired.

“We were discussing the ideal clients and the sort of clients I had.”

“Yes. Yes.”

I took a sip of my water, getting ready to summarize who an ideal client was.

"The ideal clients for StrategicEdge Marketing Solutions appreciate the value of marketing and understand that it is an investment in the growth and success of their business. They are willing to pay for quality services and results and understand that achieving marketing goals requires time, effort, and expertise. I hope you understand."

"Yes I do. Thank you."

"What you have been doing in the past is to charge incorrect fees. This has, however, caused you to obtain the worst possible clients."

Grant was clearly not pleased about his past decisions and strategies. I could tell from his disposition. I was glad he took responsibility for his decisions at least. His willingness to learn was enough proof that the company could be set back on track again.

Like my past clients who had issues with their pricing strategy, charging incorrect fees led to financial strain, reduced profitability, and difficulty in covering operating expenses and investments in growth initiatives.

I didn't want this for Grant, as much as I did want it for any of my clients. He has managed to attract clients who are difficult to work with, have unrealistic expectations, are unwilling to pay for additional services or value, or may not align with the company's target market or values.

Grant was an exceptional marketer with skills like no other. He deserved proper guidance for him to excel in his chosen field. Knowing how much he had dedicated to StrategicEdge Marketing Solutions, I wanted to see it win, now more than anything else.

"Grant, I know you have learned your lesson about setting the appropriate pricing strategy. What I do hope is that you have learned the importance of having the ideal clients and how it affects your business."

"I have, Captain. But I still have some questions in mind."

"Go ahead, Grant."

"How do I attract the ideal clients for my company?"

"It's easy. All you have to do is to be intentional about your marketing strategy."

Grant paid rapt attention, as I gave yet another insightful finance lecture.

"Clearly define the characteristics of your ideal clients, including their industry, goals, challenges, and values. This way you can tailor your marketing efforts and messaging to attract clients who are the best fit for your services."

"Hmm…."

"You will need your publicity and marketing team to develop marketing messages that resonate with your ideal clients' needs, pain points, and objectives. Highlight the unique value proposition of your services and how they can help clients achieve their goals and overcome challenges. With these methods, you should be able to attract your ideal clients."

"Thank you, Captain."

"You're always welcome, Grant."

"Quick question, Captain. With these tips you have shared with me, do you think it will be possible to attract non-ideal clients?"

"Well, of course. Those types of clients will always exist. They would also desire to do business with you, seeing the high-quality services you provide."

"Okay…."

"This is normal in business. However, you must bear in mind that while non-ideal clients may still express interest in working with your business, focusing on attracting and serving your ideal clients can lead to more successful and fulfilling partnerships in the long run."

"How, then, do I keep the wrong type of clients from my business?"

"As I said earlier, you must remain focused on your target clients. Set boundaries with clients regarding scope creep, communication frequency, and response times."

"Okay."

"In truth, you cannot cut off all non-ideal clients and stop them from approaching you. All you need is focus."

"I cannot thank you enough, Captain."

"Ohh…yes, you can. You can when you settle my bills." I joked.

We both broke into a roar of laughter. I had always been very candid about my service charge. I was never one to compromise because I understand the quality and confidentiality of my service. If it were up to me, I would be the model business owner.

"I believe I have done justice to all your questions and doubts. Or is there something I must have missed, maybe by accident or so?"

Grant and I took a minute to carefully look at his financial records and notes. It was highly possible that I had missed a crucial point, while it was my goal to cover all grounds irrespective of how negligible any part may seem.

"It seems we have covered all areas, Captain."

"Okay, good. Now let us go back to your initial question."

"Do you mean the one that brought you here, to Florida, in the first place?"

"Yes, that's the one."

"I had asked, how much do you think StrategicEdge Marketing Solutions can get from potential investors?"

I gave Grant a relaxed smile. We had gotten to a juncture where he was open-minded enough to understand the intricacies of business and finance.

"As you know right now, no sane investor would invest in StrategicEdge Marketing Solutions, at the moment. But you need not worry about that now."

"How   so?"

"How not so."

Grant gave me a confused look. I, for one, was surprised he had not gotten the main point of all our discussions by now. It seems I had to break it down to him, again. It was my job, after all.

"Grant, right now your business is worth nothing."

His response to this was a strong look, hiding all forms of emotions, including disappointment I presume.

"Your business has no worth, now. If you don't tread cautiously, you may even run into a negative balance."

"I know that."

"I know you do. And I want you to know that this is the main reason investors will not bet their money on your company."

He took a real deep breath, let out a loud exhale. He was exasperated. I understood. Anyone would be by now, even I felt the same way. But what could I do? I couldn't filter the truth. My job was to provide him, my client, with solutions.

"In order to get any serious investors, we would have to first of all work on increasing the worth of the business."

"Okay."

"Yes, that should be our goal now. We have to make the business profitable. We need your cash flow to look attractive again. That is the whole point of our conversation."

"I see."

"Making StrategicEdge Marketing Solutions viable, doesn't just bring investors, but it works in our favor as well. The huge amount you believe you need from investors might not be so necessary when your firm records its own profit."

"So, the goal is profitability."

"Yes, my good sir."

"Okay."

"To make the business profitable, you would have to apply every bit of advice and guidance I have rendered here today."

"I will."

"This is beyond affirming your position on the matter, Grant. You have to apply each point carefully for the next six months, so that in the next business year, results may begin to reflect."

"I understand."

"Still, let me break this down once again. I want to be of rested mind that you fully understand the reason for and the implications of every action you take on your business."

"Okay. Please go ahead."

"First of all, Grant, currently, we both know StrategicEdge Marketing Solutions has a weak brand image."

"Yes, we discovered that."

"I must implore you to work hard on the branding of your company. Something must come to mind when your firm comes to the mind of a potential client. And, it must be something good. Not just good, but the right image."

"Yes. We need the brand image to be a strong and reputable one."

"Exactly. Unlike most marketing firms here in Florida or Amsterdam, you should make your brand an approachable and reliable one. You do want clients to have trust in your brand. As they say, your best advertisement is one given by a satisfied client."

"Yes. Yes."

"So, make your clients happy. Not just any client, but the right ones. Remember who your ideal clients are and attract them."

"I remember who they are."

"Good. Ensure your marketing strategies align with the needs of these ideal clients." "I will

ensure just that."

"When you have proof of satisfied clients, they could even be your proof to your future investors on the reason why they would be doing right by investing in your firm."

"I see."

"Yes, exactly."

"While you aim to attract your ideal clients, you must never forget your new pricing strategy." "Hmm, that

too."

I nodded in agreement.

"You must ensure that your prices are set in such a way that it is sufficient enough to compensate you and all your staff substantially for the contributions you all make for the progress of the company."

"Okay."

"While doing that, you must also ensure your price charge is sufficient enough to cover all operational costs of running the business. However, it must also include your business profit. All of this must be put into careful consideration when setting the price."

"I understand."

"Hmm…you must be intentional about all of this. And above all, as the owner of StrategicEdge Marketing Solutions, you must ensure that every worker, including yourself, receives the appropriate reimbursement for their job. No one should be underpaid for whatever reason. All salaries must be set based on qualifications, and nothing else."

"Noted, sir."

"Good. With these, be rest assured that your business will finally pick up again. Investors will soon come trooping in."

"Thank you, Captain. I will apply everything we have talked about today. A meeting will be set up with my staff and we will discuss the implementation of these."

"Ensure that execution follows after the meeting. Do not let all that has been discussed die in the boardroom."

"I won't." He replied, reassuringly.

"Now, Grant, lighten up. You do not need all this worrying."

He smiled, but it was a halfhearted one. Clearly, he still had doubts about the possible success of his business.

"Rather than worry, I implore you to look on the bright side."

"What bright side, Captain? I do not see one in our present circumstance."

"Oh…there is one. This 'one' can lead to many." I gesticulated, communicating how exciting the one bright side was.

"What is this…bright side?" Grant curiously inquired.

"You have me." I replied, patting my chest.

It was definitely not the response he expected. A look of disappointment washed over his face.

"Listen, I mean it. Inquiring my expertise on this matter has basically saved your business. We have looked through your records. We have done our analysis. And, we spotted errors and bad business practices and strategies. Regardless, we have come up with suitable solutions for each one of these problems. So what is left?"

"Effecting the solutions."

"That's it! You have to effect these solutions. Don't sleep on it. If you address these issues, you can bounce back, get on the right track and can afford to pay the engine of the company. As complicated as it may sound, it's really simple."

"Sorry? What do you mean by engine?"

"The engine of your company is all human resources, including you, who work and contribute to the effective growth and success of StrategicEdge Marketing Solutions."

"Ohh…okay,   thanks."

"You're   most

welcome."

There was dead silence for about five minutes in the office. Grant continued staring at the computer screen. He, apparently, was studying the records again, to see if there were any more issues to address or any more questions to ask.

I, on the other hand, stared at my smartphone. I was busy, searching for an anecdote I could use to properly illustrate my final message to him, before we finally called it a day.

Yes, I had found just the right one. Grant was a smart young fella, my message will be most pellucid to him.

"Grant, can I engage you in a… a… a story?"

"A story?"

"Yes,   please."

"Alright,   you

may."   "Thank

you."

I cleared my throat, getting my results ready for my little tale.

"I once had a client. For confidentiality's sake, we'll call him Alex."

"Okay."

“Alex was an exquisite chef, one of the finest you would see in London.”

“Hmm?”

“Yes, he was. He had awards, plaques, and trophies in his name.”
“Okay.” I watched Grant's mind, surf through all the profiles of the famous chefs of London. Too bad, Alex wasn't one of them. He wasn't real.

“For a long time, almost fifteen years, Alex served other chefs in their own restaurants. He always shared with me his dream of opening a gourmet restaurant. Luckily for him, his dreams came true.”

“He opened a restaurant in London?”

“No, he moved down to the big city of Florida, and launched a fine gourmet restaurant in the heart of the city.”

“Smart man.”

“Indeed, a very smart man.”

“So how did his business fare?”

“Initially, the business went well. You know it was a one-man with very few staff assisting him. This caused him to multitask. He worked as the restaurant manager, the cook of all dishes, and he also tended to wash the dishes.”

“It must have been tiring, let alone difficult.”

“Yes, it was. Do you know what happened?”

“What?” Grant inquired with so much interest.

“He became ineffective in all of his duties. He wasn't overseeing the restaurant's operations properly, nor was he doing justice to delivering the most nectarean meal which he was known for.”

“That must have been awful.”

“Yes, it was. It was dreadful because slowly, his business began to slip away. He faced burnouts and stress-related conditions. But, he still couldn't deliver as he ought to.”

“So, what did he do about the issue?”

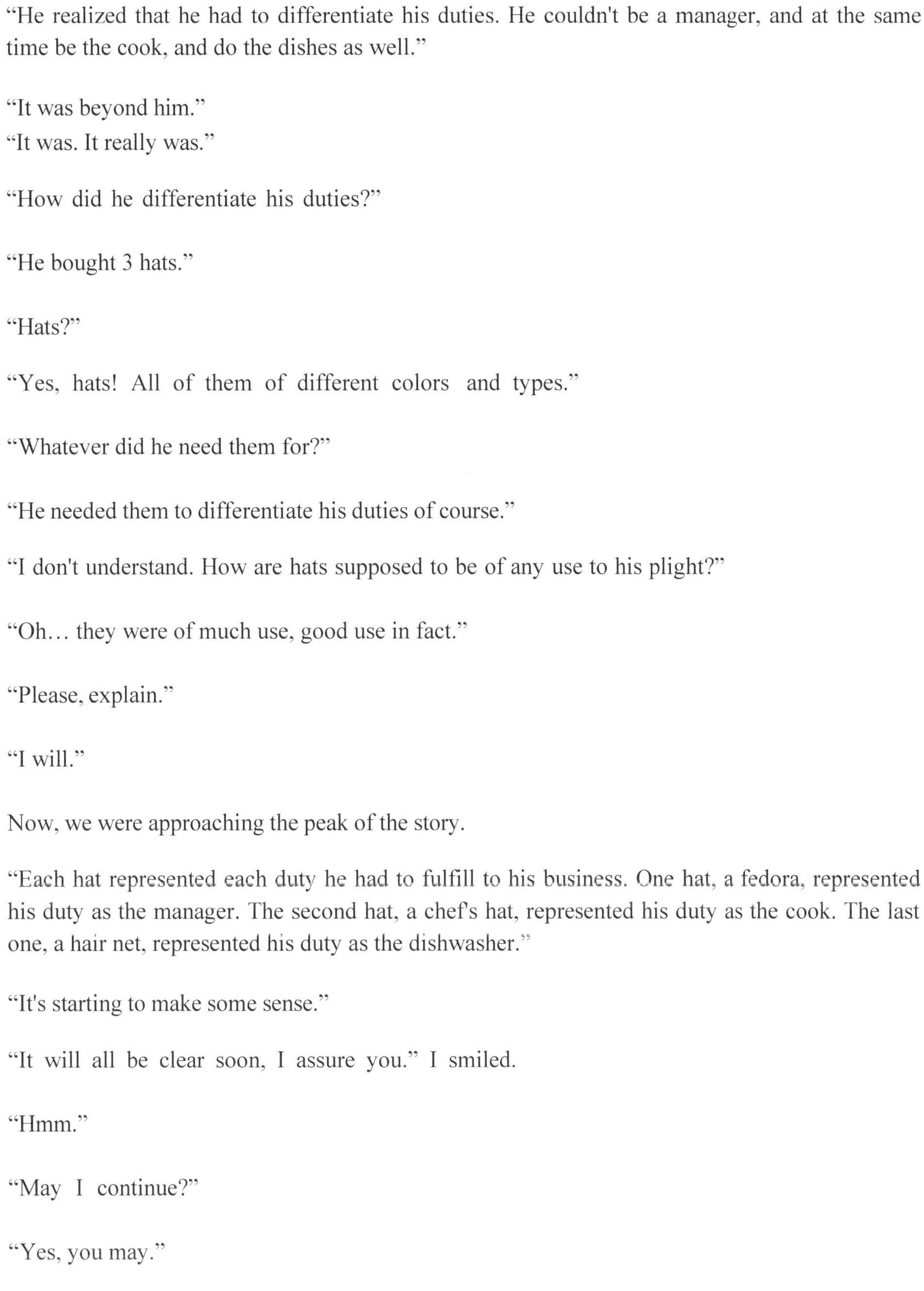

"He realized that he had to differentiate his duties. He couldn't be a manager, and at the same time be the cook, and do the dishes as well."

"It was beyond him."
"It was. It really was."

"How did he differentiate his duties?"

"He bought 3 hats."

"Hats?"

"Yes, hats! All of them of different colors and types."

"Whatever did he need them for?"

"He needed them to differentiate his duties of course."

"I don't understand. How are hats supposed to be of any use to his plight?"

"Oh… they were of much use, good use in fact."

"Please, explain."

"I will."

Now, we were approaching the peak of the story.

"Each hat represented each duty he had to fulfill to his business. One hat, a fedora, represented his duty as the manager. The second hat, a chef's hat, represented his duty as the cook. The last one, a hair net, represented his duty as the dishwasher."

"It's starting to make some sense."

"It will all be clear soon, I assure you." I smiled.

"Hmm."

"May I continue?"

"Yes, you may."

"Now, whenever Alex put on one hat, he completely neglected his other duties, focusing fully on the duty the current hat represented.”

“Ouu…smart!”
“Very smart. Whenever he was a chef with the chef's hat on, he was only a chef and nothing more. When he put on the fedora, he was only a manger. It was that simple. This enabled him to switch in and out roles easily.”

“Hmm… but who covered his duties when he wasn't available.”

“He hired an assistant for every role. These assistants, each, covered for him everytime he was unavailable.”

“He made a very smart move, I must say.”

“Yes, he did. He made a decision, one that every manager who works as an operational staff must also make.”

“Yes, indeed. Is there a way I can meet this Alex man? I believe I have a lot to learn from him.”

I laughed, breaking character so seamlessly.

“Grant, you cannot meet

Alex.” “Why?”

“Alex isn't real.”

Grant was dumbfounded. He had really taken it very seriously, which was good, in a way.

“Alex isn't real?”

“Yes, he isn't.”

“So his business, it's all made up?”

“Yes, it's all made up but not for a sham. I wanted you to learn a lesson from the anecdote.”

“I see.”

“Hmm hmm.”

“So what should my lesson be?”

“I believe I should be asking you?”

Grant chuckled.

“Let's see… I learned that as the owner of the company, I should know when to put my managerial hat on and my operational hat on.”

“That's exactly my point.”

“Thanks.”

“Look, Grant. You're an exceptional marketer. You really are. But however good you seem to be at marketing, you're bad at business management. This is the gospel truth.”

It was another bombshell dropped on Grant. But, it was his last for today.

“Do not think that because you're bad at business management now, you'll always suck at it. No, that shouldn't be your thought at all.”

“What should I think?”

“Think about improvement. People improve. Business management is a skill. As you have mastered the art of marketing, you can master business management as well.”

“I see.”

“So, the key here is not to focus solely on providing the best marketing strategies but also to be a great business manager. You shouldn't just know how to strategize, you must excel in every area of managing your business. You, as the business manager, are the pillar supporting your business.”

Now, the message of the anecdote was being made clear.

“Grant, do not think you are the only person who struggles in this area. Trust me, it is a global dilemma. It happens in a lot of businesses. The key solution is recognizing the problem and working on it. The owner is good, but their role is an operator in the business and not the manager.
Like you said earlier, you literally need 2 hats in your business, so you can step in and out of your role in the business.”

“So, I was this ‘Alex’ you spoke of.” Grant teased.

“Yes, you were.” I laughed.

“Well, Alex's business excelled in the end, didn't it?”

"Yes, it did."

"Then surely, mine

will." "I love your

confidence."

"Oh… it is you, Captain, who gave me such confidence."

In unison, we broke into a swirling fit of laughter.

"Don't worry, Grant. Like I always tell all my clients, in a year's time, you would reach out to me with good news to share."

"I really hope so."

"I hope so too."

I began to pack up my gear. I shut down my computer system, arranging my stuff in my leather suitcase. I handed Grant the flash drive, signifying the accomplished end of our session.

"Sir. Captain Number

Cruncher." Grant stood from his

seat. "Grant Wellington."

I did the same.

"It was wonderful learning from you. I hope we can do this again in the future."

"I hope so too."

"Maybe then, I would not be so novice in the business management field."

"You wouldn't be."

We both smiled, shaking our hands rigorously. Genuinely, I had enjoyed every minute of my session with Grant. He was a receptive gentleman, ready to maximize and reach his full potential.

Grant hospitably led me out of his office. We took the elevator to the reception.

"So, you plan on going back to Washington DC tomorrow?" He enquired.

"No. I would love to stay back for a week or two. It would be splendid, exploring the beautiful sceneries of Florida."

"Yes, indeed. Florida has quite a lot to offer in that aspect. I do hope you enjoy yourself."

"Yes, I will."

Deep down, I also wanted to stay back just in case Grant needed my financial expertise on any issue concerning StrategicEdge Marketing Solutions.

We stopped at the driveway. I ordered an Uber to drop me off at the hotel where I had lodged.

"Grant."

"Captain."

"Till we meet again."

"Till we meet again."

"I expect an email from you though, to keep me well-updated on your company's progress."

"I will keep you informed."

"Good luck, Grant."

"Thank you, Captain. I will be needing it."

I got into the SUV that had come to pick me up.

"Please, let me know when you're leaving for Washington." Grant's English accent yelled as the car zoomed off.

***

Grant and I kept in close touch for the few weeks I was in Florida. My much needed vacation helped me break sweat. Through our email conversations, Grant let me know of the implementation of the tips I had given him during our session. Their outcomes, as expected, were all positive. Although, on some occasions, he experienced setbacks. Nonetheless, with my guidance, and his excellent wit, he scaled through.

As I boarded the plane back home, I felt a sense of pride in Grant's progress and growth. Our partnership had blossomed into a collaborative effort fueled by mutual trust and respect. With each hurdle overcome and each success celebrated, it was clear that Grant was well on his way to achieving his goals and realizing his vision for StrategicEdge Marketing Solutions.

As for me, I returned to my home in Washington DC rejuvenated and inspired, ready to continue supporting Grant and other business owners on their journey to success. Our ongoing collaboration was a testament to the power of mentorship, guidance, and unwavering determination in the face of adversity. Together, we had proven that with the right support and mindset, any obstacle could be overcome, and any dream could be turned into reality.

It was yet another successful adventure for me, Captain Number Cruncher. I look forward to even more adventures where I help my clients increase their fortune. Maybe in the future, I will finally get the recognition that I know I deserve as the financial messiah that I am.

www.ingramcontent.com/pod-product-compliance
Lightning Source LLC
LaVergne TN
LVHW072355070726
842862LV00041B/899